THE
GENIUS OF
GIULIANI

NOTES ON
THE 120 STUDIES FOR THE RIGHT HAND
OF MAURO GIULIANI

BY HARRY GEORGE PELLEGRIN

PAB PUBLISHING © 2012

PAB Entertainment Group
P.O. Box 2369
Scotia, New York 12302
www.pellegrinlowend.com

Printed in the United States of America

GENIUS OF GIULIANI, THE

Cover designed by £ Pound Sterling Graphics

Publisher's Note: *All compositions are in the public domain except for those composed by Harry G. Pellegrin. The reproduction of the early edition of Mauro Giuliani's 120 Studies is presented with permission and by the courtesy of Statens Musikbibliotek - The Music Library of Sweden, The Carl Oscar Boije Collection*

Library of Congress Cataloging-in-Publication data is available upon request.

ISBN 978-1-105-95307-1

Pellegrin, Harry G., The Genius of Giuliani

Copyright 2012

The Genius of Giuliani

The 120 Exercises for the Right Hand, Opus One Number One, supposedly published when Mauro Giuliani was only twenty years of age*, is often either overlooked or undervalued by a great number of teachers of the classical guitar. After over 40 years of using these studies both as a daily warm-up as well as a teaching tool with my own students, I have found that I am regularly finding little jewels contained within the structure and arrangement of these tiny studies.

Maestro Giuliani designed the 120 Exercises so that the student would face only minor difficulties executing the left-hand chord shapes, thereby freeing the student to concentrate on the right hand. Indeed, I believe he wanted the student to actually *watch* the right hand. The first exercise, shown below, demonstrates the left hand shapes that the guitarist will encounter throughout the majority of the exercise. [There are a group of exercises, 101 through 110, where the left hand executes melodic passages rather than the strictly chordal arpeggiation.] The harmonic content is purely the tonic/dominant/tonic (I – V7 – I) progression (arguably the most common harmonic progression in western music.) Giuliani kept things brick-simple by choosing the key of C major – neither sharps nor flats to distract the student. Interestingly, many students find the transition to Giuliani's first-inversion G7 to be a tricky handful at first. Note: in the following examples the final c major chord of each exercise is edited from both the Vladimir Bobri edition [Celeste Publishing, New York, 1949] and Paul Brelinsky edition [Warner Brothers, Miami, Florida, 1983] to match that of the Elias Barreiro edition [The Willis Music Company, Florence, Kentucky, 1982.] In this edition, the e stopped on the second fret of the fourth string is removed. I believe Maestro Barreiro eliminated the note so that the right thumb would not have to pluck two strings—or as the Artaria edition indicates—a total shift of the right hand so that the thumb strums all five strings. [This edition, reproduced following my edition, indicates a thumb stroke for all strings beginning at the fifth string.] I prefer the *p, i, m, a* fingering, an approach which maintains a consistent right hand position throughout the exercise(s).

It is my belief that Giuliani wished the guitarist to maintain a good base-line or home position for the fingers of the right hand as follows: *p* (thumb) placed on the sixth string and 'covering' the three bass strings (6th, 5th and 4th) with the *i* (index) placed upon the third string, *m* (middle) on the second string and *a* (ring) on the first string. So, why then does Giuliani's first exercise begin with the *i* and *m* fingers covering the first and second strings? I am convinced that Giuliani insisted upon this fingering as it would be most simple for the new student to use two 'strong' fingers (*i* and *m*); he may have thought *m* and *a* to possibly be a daunting combination for the student as the *a* finger is rather weak for  most students. In short, I believe he wished to be as 'low-impact' as possible when introducing his exercises. However, the alternative fingering as shown in Paul Brelinsky's edition of these exercises is arguably more in accord with the concept of a home position for the right hand (see next musical sample):

•   Some sources state that Giuliani reserved his Opus One for his pedagogical works and that these were
    published well into his performing, teaching and publishing career.

Even so, note that the thumb is extended over to the third string! [Example above] Ideal execution of the exercise using perfect home-positioning would result in the following fingering—one that might be difficult to cleanly execute for the new student [Example below]:

To support my premise of a base-line position that minimizes right hand motion and maintains hand geometry, I draw attention to exercises 13 and 18. In these exercises, the right hand thumb (*p*) covers the fifth and fourth strings and the index finger (*i*) is solely responsible for the third string, with the middle (*m*) and ring (*a*) fingers exclusively covering the second and first strings respectively:

Exercises one through three allow the student to acclimate to the left hand chord-shapes as well as to the concept of moving the thumb to 'cover' the fifth and fourth strings. The index and middle fingers remain static, whether used in block intervals or to arpeggiate the two notes consigned to their execution.

It is in exercise four that Giuliani introduces the student to the concept that to successfully finger certain melodic/harmonic passages, the right hand will have to, by necessity, leave the 'home' positioning. By doing so, fingers will be used to pluck strings not covered by their standard home position location. Note in exercise four that the index and middle finger 'track' with the thumb. In other words, the two fingers are placed on the fourth (*i*) and third (*m*) string as the thumb plucks the fifth, then all three digits are relocated to the fourth (*p*) third (*i*) and second (*m*), then the third (*p*), second (*i*) and first (*m*). (See exercise four below.)

Exercise five is the same framework as exercise four but with the order of *p*, *i* and *m* changed to *m*, *i* and *p*. Giuliani's *modus operandi* is to create an exercise and then modify it. (Compare exercises one through three, four and five, as well as seven and eight to see the variation techniques Giuliani uses.)

Exercise seven is the first exercise to strictly enforce the 'home position' concept. Here the student is first introduced to the concept that ***non-adjacent strings are plucked with non-adjacent fingers while adjacent strings are plucked by adjacent fingers***. Note: The thumb is, strictly speaking, *not* a finger. The thumb is the digit that opposes the fingers. Suffice to say, the thumb can be considered an adjacent finger to the index finger as well as a non-adjacent finger to the index finger when discussing right hand guitar technique. Its range of motion can be brought close to the index finger or remain at a distance without changing basic hand geometry.

Exercise Seven:

Notice that on beat one of the first measure the thumb is used as a non-adjacent finger in regard to the index finger. The thumb is on the fifth string while the index finger is on the third string –normal home-position placement. On beat two, the thumb is used as an adjacent finger to the index finger, covering strings four and three respectively. Giuliani introduces another technical issue at this juncture: The thumb is now required to extend to cover the sixth string on beat three of measure two. From this point onward, Giuliani will often use the root note on the third beat of measure two of the exercises.

I believe that Giuliani wished the student to play all 120 exercises in a single session once they had been learned. With repeats, the 120 exercises can be cleanly executed in about ten minutes with no great strain or undue pressure. A sustained tempo is indicated for the entire session as it is apparent that

Giuliani 'built in' increases in tempo. Look at exercise seven on the previous page.   Note the order of arpeggiation and the required right hand fingering. Compare this with exercise thirty three. It is easy to see that the exercise is identical in both arpeggiation as well as fingering. It has been rendered twice as long—and twice as fast in tempo—by changing the eighth notes triplets to sixteenth note sextuplets.

Therefore, the student must begin the exercises at a somewhat slower tempo than might otherwise be indicated by the block-chord nature of exercise one. Do not be concerned if this seems too slow, Maestro Giuliani will speed things up! These exercises can be broken down into groups determined by the type of treatment the chords receive:

BLOCK:

STANDARD ARPEGGIO:

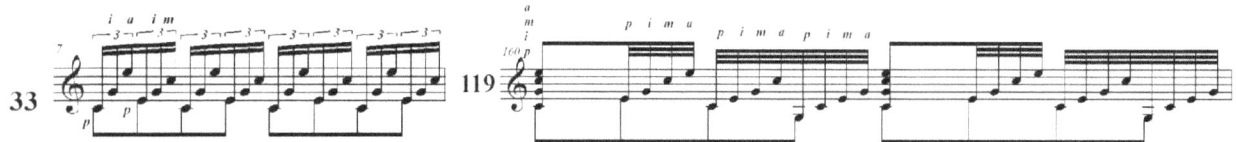

MELODIC/CHORDAL HYBRID:

The guitarist should perform these studies as required to hone and maintain proper right hand geometry and technique. No one ever 'gets past' these exercises or comes to the point where he or she cannot gain more from continued practice. These exercises can be used to improve tone, perfect the accenting of various fractions of the beat, to correct rhythmic inaccuracy as well as a myriad of other technical issues.

Giuliani's studies are wonderfully arranged. He does not touch upon one technical aspect, exhaust it, and then leave for a new series of exercises; he revisits technical concepts, and at a quicker tempo created by the use of ever smaller note values. The aforementioned 'built-in' speed increase is the basis for my premise that he intends the guitarist to play all 120 exercises in one session—he builds in complexity and builds in speed so that the guitarist starts at a slow comfortable pace and technical level and progresses gradually to complexity and speed. By doing this, he prevents the student from either becoming totally bored or from forgetting or ignoring previously acquired skills. It should take the experienced guitarist less than ten minutes to complete the 120 right hand studies.

This is the genius of Giuliani, a factor that is either neglected or forgotten by many of today's pedagogues: these exercises are not merely a collection of isolated examples of arpeggiations that one might find in the repertoire; rather they are a single, cohesive study. These 120 studies represent a very low-impact warm up for the right hand. Coupled with the practice of scales as part of a warm-up regimen, both the right as well as the left hand will be warmed, exercised and developed. Recommended scales are the Diatonic Major and Minor Scales as fingered by Andrés Segovia. (1953, Columbia Music Company, Theodore Presser Co., King of Prussia, PA. Catalog Number: CO127)

The following edition of Giuliani's 120 Studies for the Right Hand is taken from my Classic Guitar Method (2006-2012, PAB Publishing, PO Box 2369 Scotia, New York, 12302 ISBN: 978-0-557-26825-2) and includes small changes in right hand fingering I have made to keep the right hand in the previously described home-position. Following my edition is a facsimile reprint of the Artaria (Vienna) second edition of the studies. This is furnished by permission from, and through the courtesy of Statens Musikbibliotek - The Music Library of Sweden, The Carl Oscar Boije Collection of historic guitar sheet music, to whom I wish to express my most sincere gratitude. I have included this significant document so that the serious student can compare my edition to a source close to the original.

On to the studies!

The student should select a tempo in exercise one that allows for a clean execution of exercise one hundred-twenty. In other words, the tempo never increases or decreases throughout the exercises. If one plays the first exercise at 100 beats-per-minute, I can almost state with certainty that the performance will come to a crashing halt by exercise twenty-six!

In preparation for Giuliani's 120 Right Hand Studies the student must be able to transition between the C Major and G 7 (first inversion) chord shapes. Practice the following exercise at a speed that allows for clean, accurate and EVEN transitions between the chords. When this exercise can be played to perfection, move on to the Giuliani exercises.

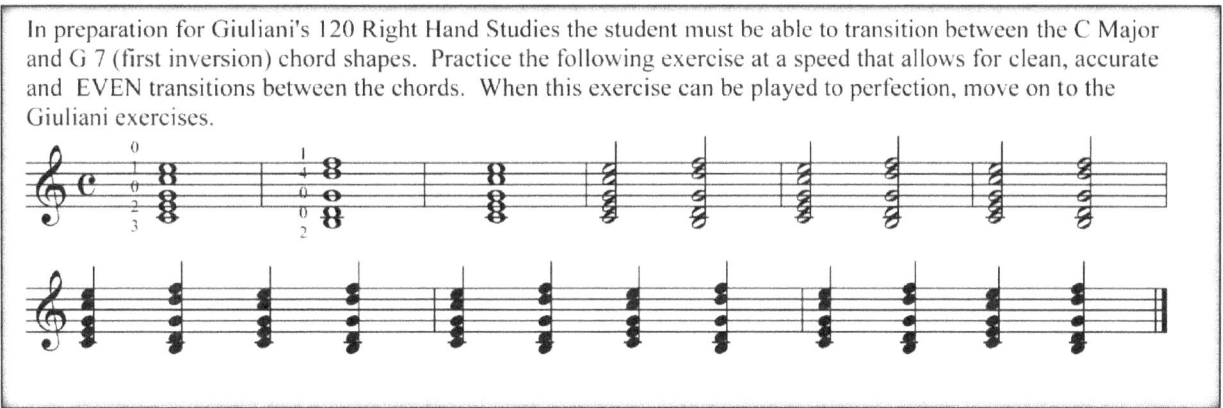

Studies One through Six:

These are preliminary exercises. Giuliani introduces the student to the chords that will be used throughout the 120 studies with only a few modifications (exercises 101 through 108 hold the most significant of these modifications.) The student should use non-home-position right hand fingerings with the index finger and middle finger covering the first and second strings in exercises one through three. Exercise one is a simple block iteration of the two chords, I and V7 in C major. Exercises two and three arpeggiate exercise one in the simplest manner. Exercise four introduces positional right hand play. In other words, the thumb, index and middle fingers play the adjacent strings and then move to another set of three adjacent strings. This style of arpeggiation lasts through exercise six. Exercise six contains an interesting problem for the new student. A note is repeated; however the right hand plucks the repeated note with a different finger. Many students attempt to pluck the second (repeated) note with the same finger.

Studies Seven through Twenty-four:

Giuliani introduces the student to right hand home-position fingering. In other words, the thumb covers the three wound strings while the *i* finger is responsible for all notes on the third (g) string, the *m* finger for all notes on the second (b) string and the *a* finger for the first (e) string. Exercise seven is the perfect example of this assignment of fingers. At exercise eleven, a second simultaneously plucked note is introduced to the student. The index, middle and ring finger will be in direct opposition to the thumb in various arrangements. Exercises eighteen through twenty-four are block style arpeggios.

Studies Twenty-five through Thirty-five:

These exercises are once again in standard arpeggio form. They cover much of the same material that was revealed to the student in the first ten exercises. Observe that the durations of the pitches have been decreased to sixteenth notes. This is a built-in speed increase. Although the tempo remains the same, the number of notes that must be successfully executed has doubled.

Studies Thirty-Six through Fifty:

A repetitive pattern bass is executed with the thumb and index finger, still in perfect home position play. Giuliani's edition indicates that the middles finger plucks the upper voice single note on the first string. This leads to an uncomfortable stretching apart of the index and middle fingers when they are employed simultaneously. A more real-world friendly home-position fingering would be to employ the ring finger for these upper voice notes. Remember this rule for good fingering: ***Non-adjacent fingers for non-adjacent strings; adjacent fingers play adjacent strings.***

Studies Fifty-One through Sixty-five:

Block chord arpeggios are employed once again. The bass line is straight from exercise one. The chordal upper voice, once again, is indicated in non-home-position, just like the first exercise. Play these using *i, m* and *m,a*. It is important that the student counts these exercises very carefully. The bass line shifts under the chordal accompaniment. An education on accenting various parts of the beats can be gleaned from this series of exercises.

Studies Sixty-six through Eighty:

These exercises revisit thirty-six through fifty with a slightly more complex bass line—one that incorporates the same bass line as in exercise one through three. A block chordal style upper voice once again shifts through various parts of the beat.

Studies Eighty-one through One hundred:

Once again, we are revisiting some old ground but with a few new wrinkles. Exercise eighty-nine includes a repeated finger – the thumb on the ascending side of an arpeggio and the index finger on the descending. This pattern is repeated as part of exercise ninety-one. Exercise ninety-two and ninety-three include a change to the two left-hand chord shapes that have been used since page one. The G on the sixth string is played with the fourth finger from the first beat of both measures of each exercise. The right hand is fingered so that the hand executes each finger in order (either *p,i,m,a or a,m,i,p*, and then the hand is moved to the next group of four strings to execute the following beat. Exercise one hundred introduces a form of tremolo: *p,a,m,i* followed by *p,i,m,a*.{Standard tremolo–if one can use the word in this case—is most often performed tremolo *p,i,m,a*.]

Studies One hundred-one through One hundred-ten:

These exercises finally break with the left hand chord formula the student has been using since exercise one. These exercises are melodic in nature with chromaticisms as well as scalar passages. Quite often, only one left-hand finger will remain planted while the other fingers execute the remaining melodic content. Exercise one hundred-ten includes a two-finger tremolo.

Studies One hundred-eleven through one hundred-twenty:

A student once told me these exercises looked to be the scariest of the bunch! Yes, there are intimidating groups of thirty-second notes. It is my opinion that these last exercises are easier than the previous group of melodic studies (Studies one hundred-one through one hundred-ten.) The secret is to grab the entire chord in either measure of each study—including the G on the sixth string. In exercises one-hundred-twelve and one hundred-thirteen the player must execute a full barré at the first fret, lifting the finger to play open string notes, while keeping the remainder of the barré down on the first string. The right-hand fingering is not daunting at all if one has completed the previous exercises!

Performance Notes:

Please feel free to use the alternate chord voicing for the terminal measure of each exercise as demonstrated in the earlier examples (requiring only *p, i, m, a* to cleanly perform the resulting four-note chord. One can use either *p, p, i, m, a* to execute the five-note chord as printed OR use the upward thumb glissando (bass to treble) as Maestro Giuliani recommended in his Artaria edition.

Alternate right hand fingerings are offered for some exercises. Use the indicated fingerings until these have been mastered *then* incorporate the alternate fingerings. As with any technical exercise, pay particular attention to tone and volume—it is too easy to neglect these crucial ingredients when attempting an unfamiliar passage. Practice with a metronome and be particularly careful to make triplets a true triple division of one beat and those sixteenth notes do indeed fit sixteen to a measure! Many students merely adjust tempo so that triplets and sixteenths remain constant—at the expense of uniform tempo.

As stated elsewhere, I believe Giuliani intended for the experienced player to run through all one hundred-twenty exercises in one sitting. I will reiterate: By using all the repeats, but eliminating the final block chord, it should take less than ten minutes to accomplish this.

For practice after all 120 exercises have been mastered: First practice ten a day in order. When this becomes a simple task, practice the exercises in themed groupings, i.e.: twenty five through thirty five and fifty one through sixty five. Practice contrasting groupings.

Special thanks to William Hemmings for editorial services and friendship!

Mauro Giuliani's Right Hand Exercises

Mauro Giuliani
Ed. H.G. Pellegrin

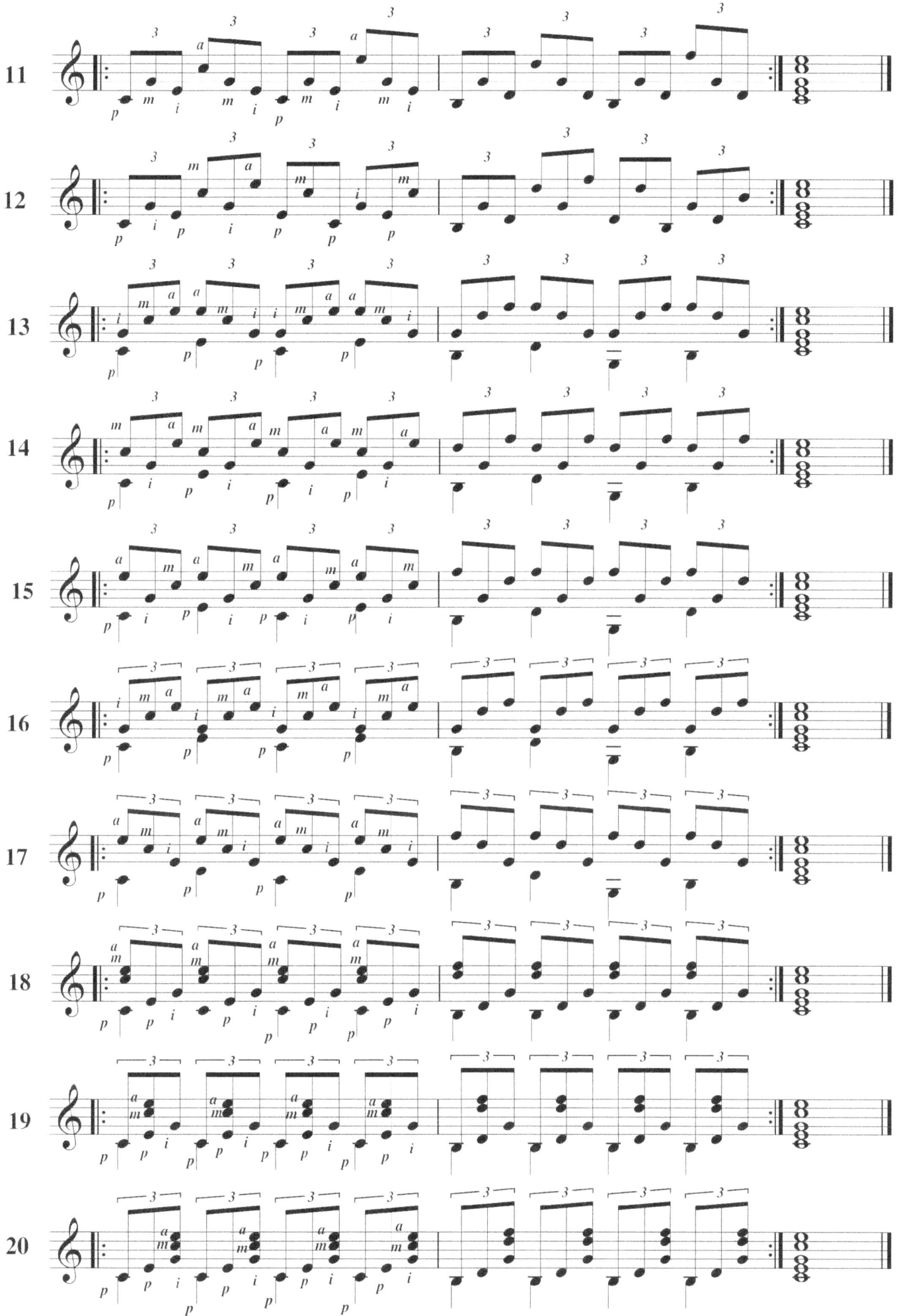

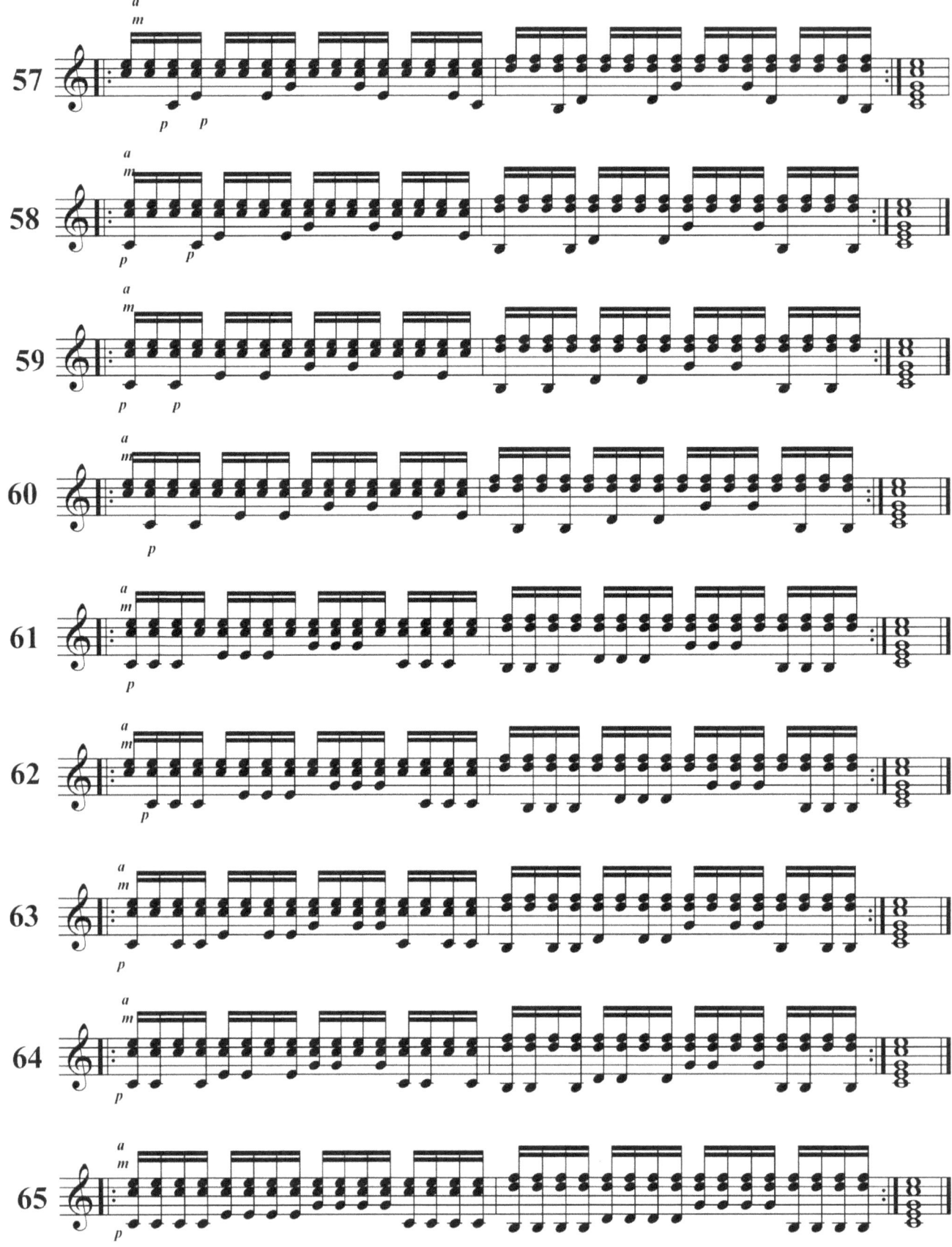

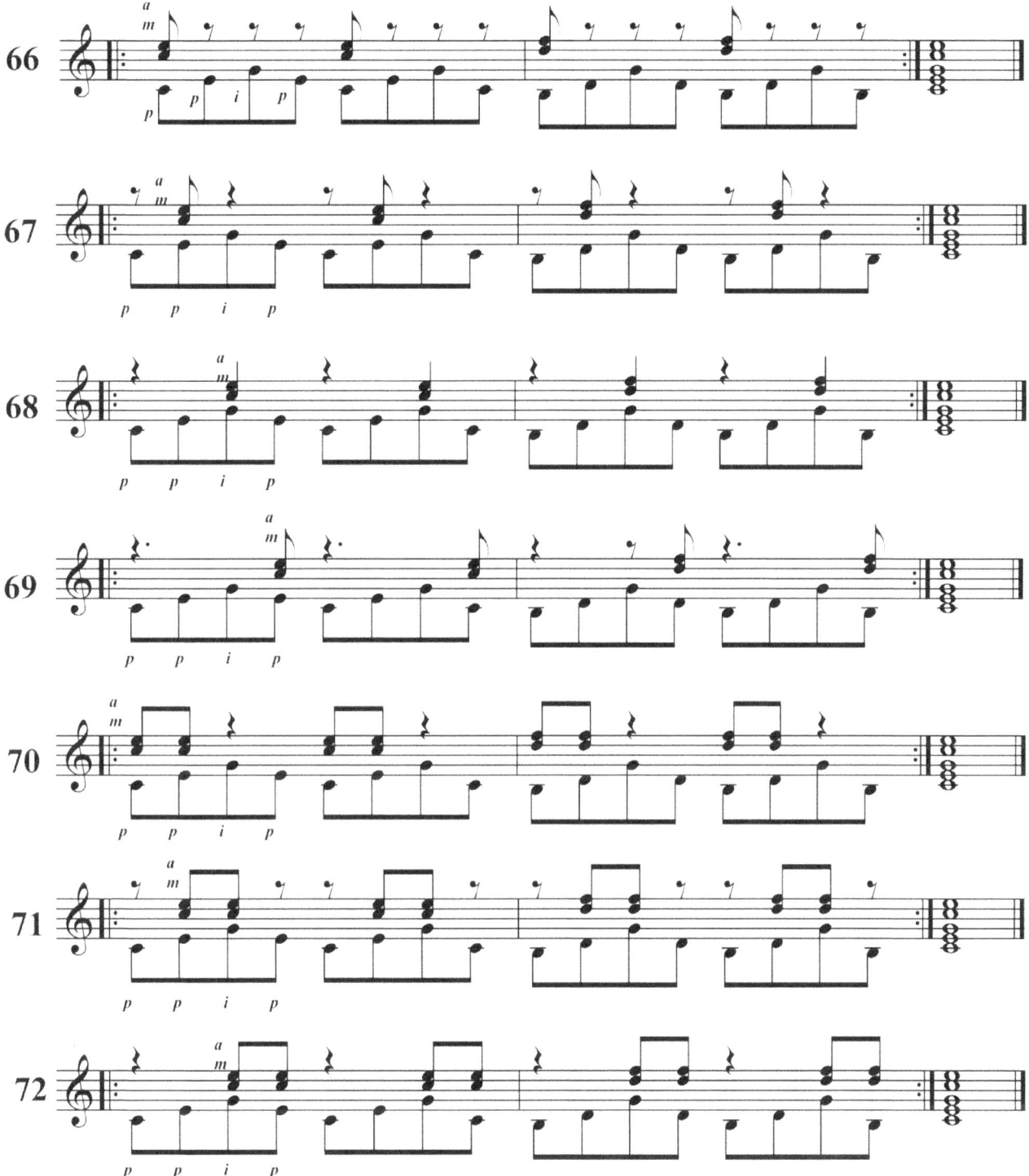

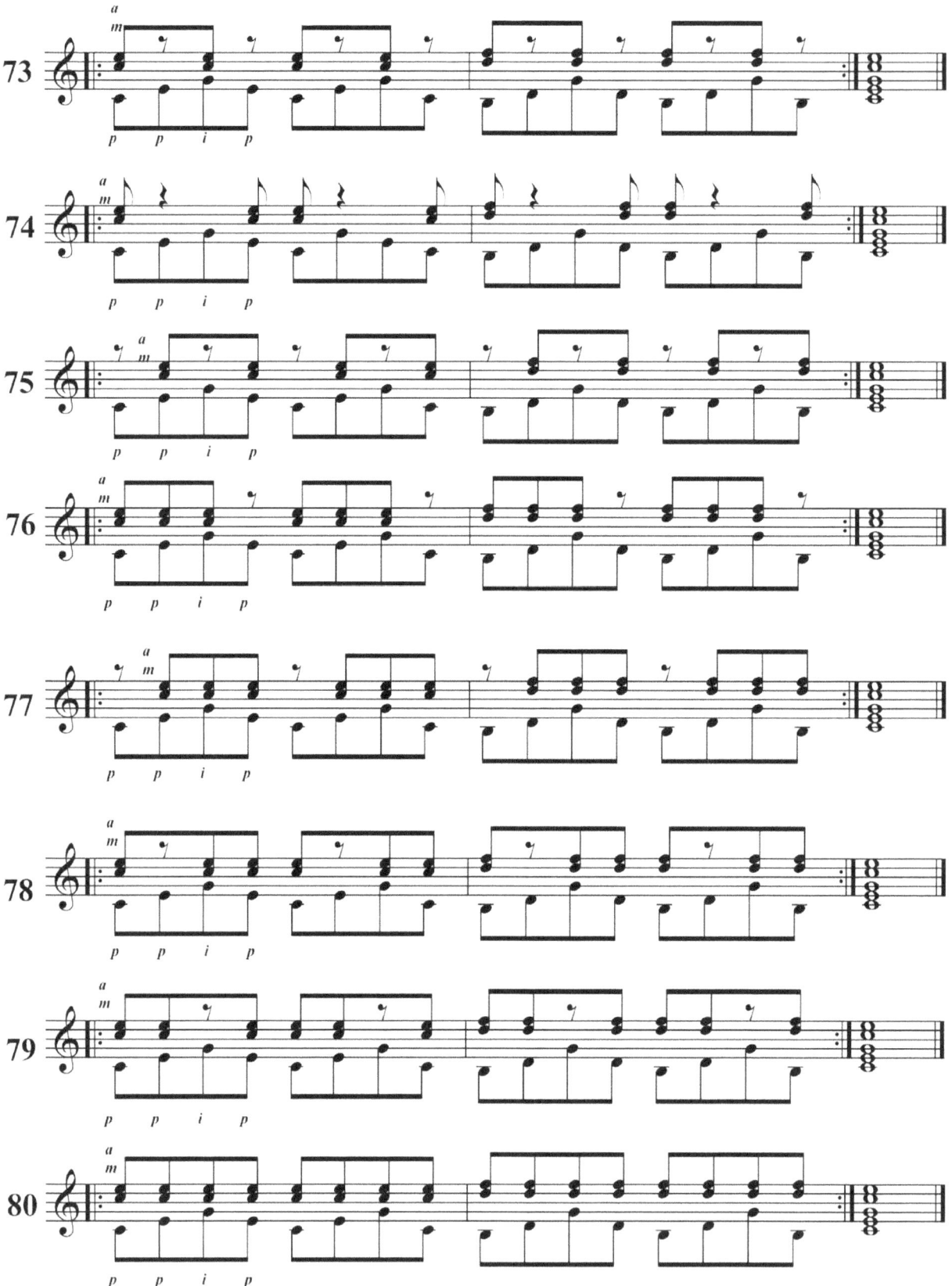

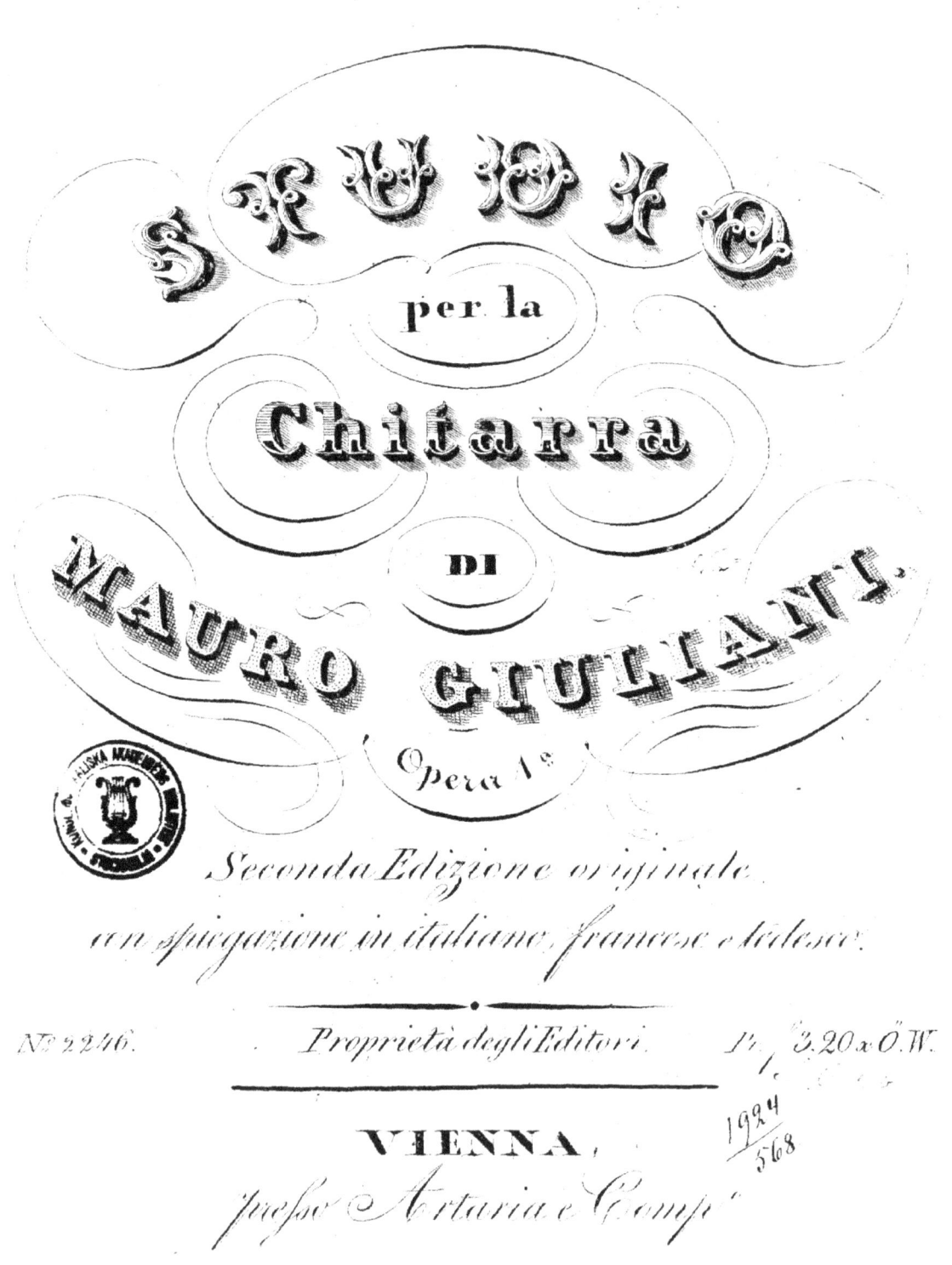

STUDIO
per la
Chitarra
DI
MAURO GIULIANI.
Opera 1.

Seconda Edizione originale
con spiegazione in italiano, francese e tedesco.

N° 2246.   Proprietà degli Editori   Pr. 3.20 x Ö.W.

1924
568

VIENNA
presso Artaria e Comp.

PRIMA PARTE | PREMIÈRE PARTIE | ERSTER THEIL

Degli arpeggi | Des arpèges | Uibung im Harpeggiren
Esercizio per la mano destra | Exercice pour la main droite | für die rechte Hand

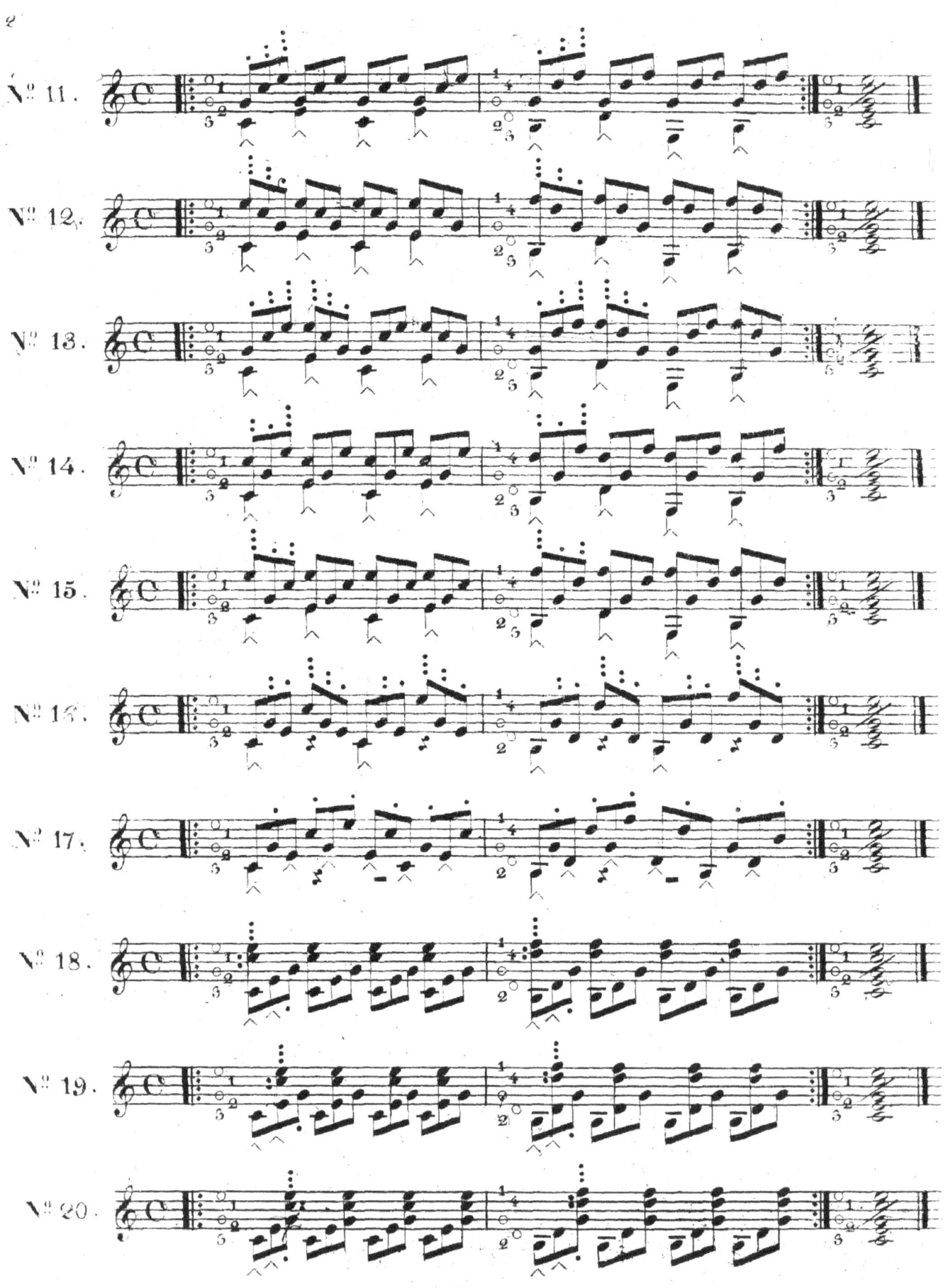

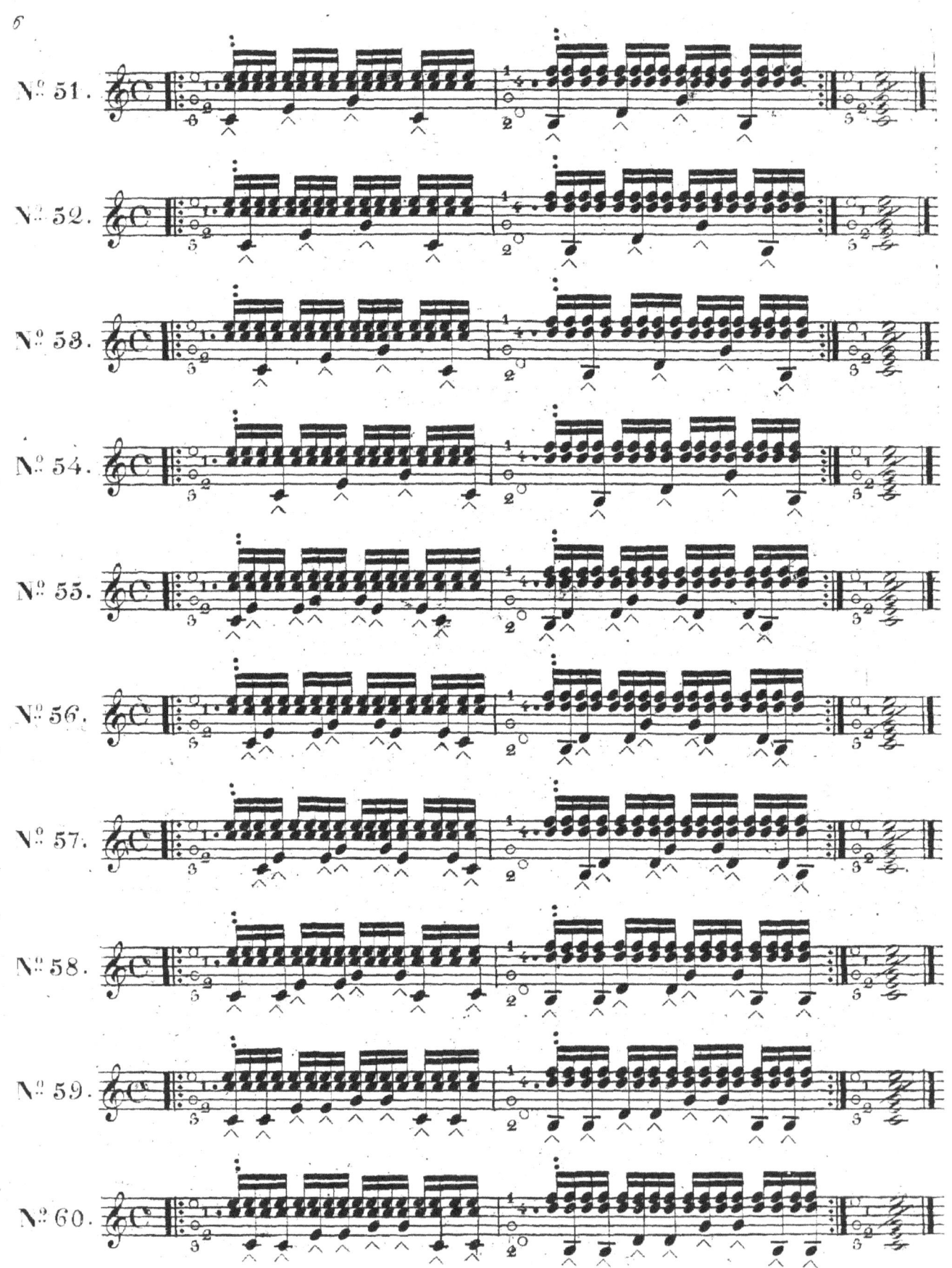

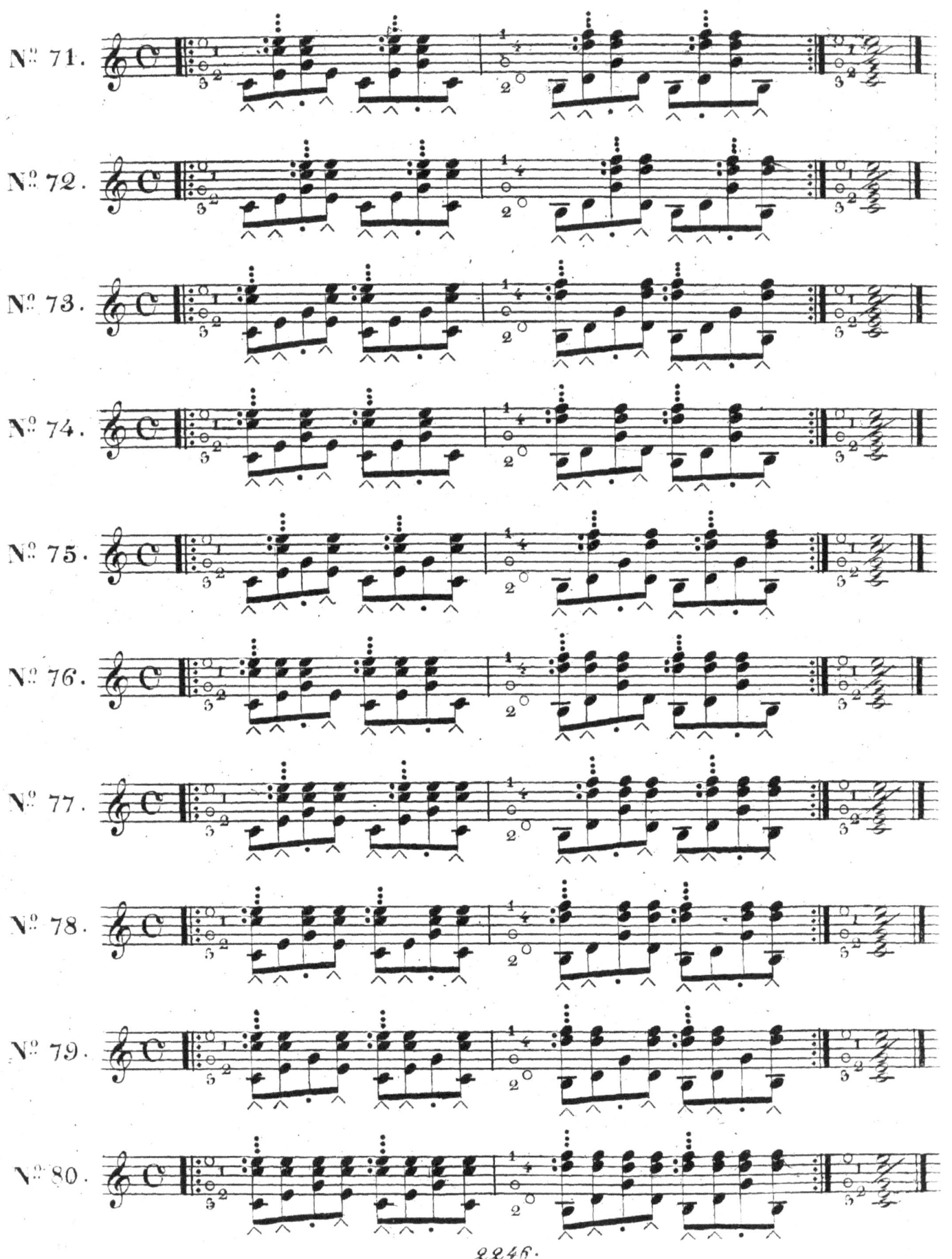

N.º 81.

N.º 82.

N.º 83.

N.º 84.

N.º 85.

N.º 86.

N.º 87.

N.º 88.

N.º 89.

N.º 90.

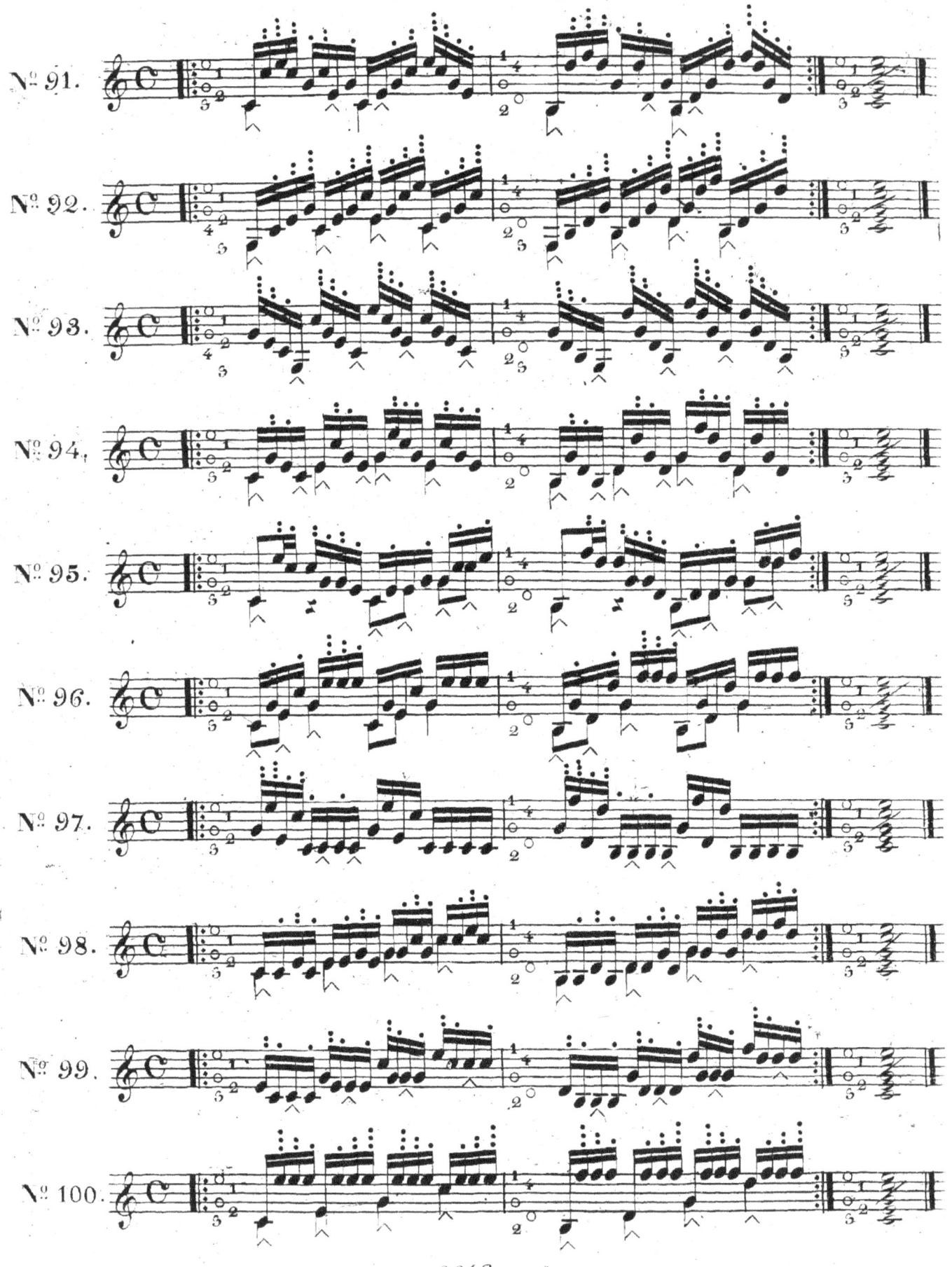

No. 91.
No. 92.
No. 93.
No. 94.
No. 95.
No. 96.
No. 97.
No. 98.
No. 99.
No. 100.

N.º 101.

N.º 102.

N.º 103.

N.º 104.

N.º 105.

N.º 106.

N.º 107.

N.º 108.

N.º 109.

N.º 110.

2246.

MAURO GIULIANI (27 July 1781 – 8 May 1828)

Giuliani is reckoned by many to be one of the leading guitar composers and virtuosos of the 19th century. Although born in Bisceglie, Giuliani's center of study was in Barletta where he moved with his brother Nicola. His first instrumental training was on the cello—an instrument which he never completely abandoned—and he probably also studied the violin. Subsequently he devoted himself to the guitar, becoming a very skilled performer on it in a short time.

In Vienna he became acquainted with the classical instrumental style. Giuliani would propel the guitar away from the simple chordal accompaniment of folk songs. In 1807 Giuliani had begun to publish compositions in the Viennese classical style. His concert tours took him all over Europe, and wherever he went he was acclaimed for his virtuosity and, as importantly, his musical style and sophistication. He achieved great success and became a musical celebrity, arguably equal to the best of the many instrumentalists and composers who were active in Vienna in the opening years of the 19th century.

Giuliani defined a new role for the guitar in the context of European music. He was well acquainted with the brightest luminaries of Austrian musical culture and with such noted composers as Rossini and Beethoven, and often worked and collaborated with the best active concert musicians in Vienna.

While in Vienna, Giuliani had some minor success as a composer. He worked mostly with the publisher Artaria, who published the large part of his works for guitar, but he had dealings with all the other local publishers, who spread his compositions all over Europe. He developed a teaching reputation as well.

In 1819 Giuliani left Vienna, mainly for financial reasons: it appears that his property and bank accounts had been confiscated to pay his debtors. He returned to Italy, spending time in Trieste and Venice, and finally settling in Rome. There he did not have much success; he published a few compositions and gave only one concert.

Four years later he returned to Naples to care for his seriously ill father. In Naples Giuliani would find a better reception to his guitar artistry than he had in Rome, and in Naples he was able to publish works for guitar with local publishers. Toward the end of 1828 the health of the musician began to fail; he died in Naples on the 8th of May, 1829.

As a guitar composer he was very fond of the *theme and variations* form— a musical device that had been extremely popular in Vienna. He had a remarkable ability to weave a melody into a passage with musical effect while remaining true to the idiom of the instrument. One example of this ability is to be found in his Variations on a theme of Handel, Op. 107. This popular theme, known as "The Harmonious Blacksmith", appears in the *Aria* from Handel's Suite No. 5 in F for harpsichord. Giuliani completed 150 compositions for guitar with opus number. These compositions constitute the core of the guitar repertoire during the 18th century. He composed extremely challenging pieces for solo guitar.

Notable pieces that stand out from his body of works include his three guitar concertos (Op. 30, 36 and 70); six fantasias for solo guitar, Op. 119-124, based on airs from Rossini operas and entitled the "Rossiniane"; several sonatas for violin and guitar and flute and guitar; a quintet, Op. 65, for strings and guitar; some collections for voice and guitar, and a Grand Overture written in the Italian style. He also transcribed many symphonic works. Even in the Twenty-first Century, Giuliani's concertos and solo pieces are performed by professionals and still demonstrate the guitarist's mastery of technique and musical eloquence, as well as Giuliani's stellar compositional gifting for the guitar.

Harry George Pellegrin was born February 4, 1957 in Bronxville, New York, United States.

Musician, writer, photographer, and graphic artist. The only child of Harry Pellegrin (1902-1981) and Veronica M. Pellegrin (1918-2004), Harry G. Pellegrin attended Mount Saint Michael Academy in the Bronx, graduating in 1974. Pellegrin studied piano as a small child but became interested in the guitar in 1970 and by 1973 was performing. Pellegrin attended Bronx Community College from 1974 to 1976. He majored in classical guitar at The Mannes College of Music in Manhattan, studying with Albert Valdés-Blain and Eliot Fisk.

A severe traffic accident in 1989 resulting in fractured thoracic and lumbar vertebrae with some permanent damage to the spine and the associated neurological deficits curtailed his musical career for almost seven years and channeled his energies towards his other interests, writing and photography. Pellegrin wrote for *Soundboard, The Journal of the Guitar Foundation of America* and *Ironhorse Magazine* before publishing his first novel *Low End*, in 2003. The first of a series, *Low End* (ISBN 1589820746) was followed by *Deep End* (ISBN 1435721985) in 2006. *Classic Guitar Method, A Comprehensive Method designed to transform the student from novice to recitalist* (ISBN 978-0-557-26825-2) combined Pellegrin's writing skills with his musical expertise. Pellegrin performed his come-back recital at the Troy Savings Bank Music Hall in Troy, New York on February 13, 2007, his first classical performance since the 1989 accident.

In May 2008 PAB Entertainment Group released *The Guitar* (700261240428) a CD of solo classical guitar music performed by Mr. Pellegrin which includes a number of compositions by the performer. In 2010 PAB released his second album of solo classical guitar *Old and New* (885767622234) which includes favorites of his from a number of stylistic periods. Pellegrin also composed and recorded a series of four brief waltzes for this CD, two of which are dedicated to his parents and celebrate their lives and chronicle his sense of loss at their deaths.

Now residing in Northern New York State with his wife and daughter, Pellegrin performs, teaches and writes. Since January 2008 he has been a member of the adjunct faculty of Union College in Schenectady, New York. He was installed as a member of the Board of Directors of the CGSUNY for calendar year 2012 and is an artist member of the Monday Musical Club of Albany.

Now in one volume, much of what the novice classical guitarist will need to know to lead him or her to the recital stage. From proper instrument care and maintenance to the necessary technical skills, musical mind-set, and the standard repertoire—all are exposed and explored with enough detail and insight that the student will wish to keep this book handy years to come as a ready reference source. With the aid of a good teacher, the student will rapidly progress through Classic Guitar Method attaining technical proficiency and musical eloquence. A number of studies by Sor, Giuliani, Coste, Carulli and Carcassi are expanded and graded. Examples from the standard repertoire reinforce the techniques highlighted in the studies.

ISBN: 978-1-4116-9442-2

Folio For Guitar is a collection of pieces for solo classical guitar that include four Vals Brevis (Brief Waltzes) as well as three tone poems: Elaine, Nacht Tanz and Snowfall: 12.28.2008. All pieces written by recitalist and composer Harry George Pellegrin. Difficulty level: intermediate to difficult.

Low End is an exciting new novel dealing with modern issues in the style of the classic 1940's mystery writers. Low End is murder mystery with a twist involving a least-likely detective, a disillusioned, New York City musician named Gary Morrissey. Gary finds himself involved in a murder investigation of his own making when shadows of government corruption and hints of premeditated genocide are cast over a friend's murder. The author's own experiences are reflected in his lead character, whose love for New York City and for its less-than-attractive suburbs and citizens emanates from every page and whose musical knowledge and expertise provide a unique background for the events that unfold. Some mild language and violence, no sex.

ISBN: 978-1-4357-2198-2

Helen is the kind of girl you dream about. She's smart and confident, funny and affectionate, and she's killer good-looking. Gary has fallen for her, and fallen hard. Even so, he is still distracted by life's little happenstances. It's those minor things like, oh, crooked cops, shady club owners, illegal smuggling, and a few dead bodies. Still, Gary can't keep his eyes off Helen. Harry Pellegrin's mystery novel DEEP END is packed with eerily real sinister characters, music, interesting locales, bizarre spirituality and a plethora of corpses. Couple this with an exceedingly clever plot and we have this year's best beach-read. Serial killings and alternative spirituality discussed. Some violence, no profanity, no sex.

ISBN: 1589820746